August 20

Dear my sister and
friend, N

You are so dear to my
heart. I love your sisterly
care   for me and

199
Promises
of God

your desire to see me to
continually grow in our
Lord. I am so proud of
how you are going to
Hungary in faith,
knowing God has asked
you to go. May these
promises of God bless
you as they've blessed
me. Kisses! Love Emily

xoxo

199
Promises
of God

BARBOUR
PUBLISHING

© 2007 by Barbour Publishing, Inc.

ISBN 978-1-59789-704-4

All scripture quotations are taken from the King James Version of the Bible.

Published by Barbour Publishing, Inc., P.O. Box 719, Uhrichsville, Ohio 44683, www.barbourbooks.com

Our mission is to publish and distribute inspirational products offering exceptional value and biblical encouragement to the masses.

Member of the
Evangelical Christian
Publishers Association

Printed in the United States of America.

INTRODUCTION

It's often easy to get weighed down with the disappointments and challenges of life. Without realizing it, our hearts become heavy and our hope for a fulfilling life turns sour.

In His kindness, God has provided uplifting promises of help and encouragement for His children within the pages of His Word, the Bible. Whatever our needs, we can find in scripture the principles we need to address the issues we face.

This collection of Bible verses is the perfect everyday pick-me-up. This book is not intended to replace regular, personal Bible study. It is, however, a quick guide to dozens of the most uplifting scriptures in the Bible. We hope it will be an encouragement to you as you read.

All scripture is taken from the King James Version of the Bible.

1

Therefore if any man be in Christ,
he is a new creature: old things are passed away;
behold, all things are become new.
2 CORINTHIANS 5:17

2

And the prayer of faith shall save the sick,
and the Lord shall raise him up; and if he
have committed sins, they shall be forgiven him.
JAMES 5:15

3

For the which cause I also suffer these things:
nevertheless I am not ashamed:
for I know whom I have believed,
and am persuaded that he is able
to keep that which I have committed
unto him against that day.

2 TIMOTHY 1:12

4

The LORD is my light and my salvation;
whom shall I fear?
the LORD is the strength of my life;
of whom shall I be afraid?

PSALM 27:1

5

The Lord is gracious, and full of compassion;
slow to anger, and of great mercy.
Psalm 145:8

6

And the Lord shall help them, and deliver them:
he shall deliver them from the wicked,
and save them, because they trust in him.
Psalm 37:40

7

For this God is our God for ever and ever:
he will be our guide even unto death.
Psalm 48:14

8

Submit yourselves therefore to God.
Resist the devil, and he will flee from you.
Draw nigh to God, and he will draw nigh to you.
Cleanse your hands, ye sinners; and purify your
hearts, ye double minded.
JAMES 4:7–8

9

He that trusteth in his own heart is a fool:
but whoso walketh wisely,
he shall be delivered.
PROVERBS 28:26

10

But as it is written,
Eye hath not seen, nor ear heard,
neither have entered into the heart of man,
the things which God hath prepared
for them that love him.

1 CORINTHIANS 2:9

11

And Jesus said unto them,
I am the bread of life:
he that cometh to me shall never hunger;
and he that believeth on me shall never thirst.

JOHN 6:35

12

For which cause we faint not;
but though our outward man perish,
yet the inward man is renewed day by day.
For our light affliction, which is but for a
moment, worketh for us a far more
exceeding and eternal weight of glory.
2 CORINTHIANS 4:16–17

13

The lip of truth shall be established for ever:
but a lying tongue is but for a moment.
PROVERBS 12:19

14

The meek shall eat and be satisfied:
they shall praise the Lord that seek him:
your heart shall live for ever.

PSALM 22:26

15

But thus saith the Lord,
Even the captives of the mighty shall be
taken away, and the prey of the terrible shall
be delivered: for I will contend with him that
contendeth with thee, and I will save thy children.

ISAIAH 49:25

16

And they that know thy name
will put their trust in thee: for thou,
Lord, hast not forsaken them that seek thee.
Psalm 9:10

17

As newborn babes,
desire the sincere milk of the word,
that ye may grow thereby.
1 Peter 2:2

18

The LORD is nigh unto them
that are of a broken heart;
and saveth such as be of a contrite spirit.
PSALM 34:18

19

And they said, Believe on the Lord Jesus Christ,
and thou shalt be saved, and thy house.
ACTS 16:31

20

For by grace are ye saved through faith;
and that not of yourselves:
it is the gift of God.
EPHESIANS 2:8

21

The Lord giveth wisdom:
out of his mouth cometh
knowledge and understanding.
He layeth up sound wisdom for the righteous:
he is a buckler to them that walk rightly.
PROVERBS 2:6–7

22

For he shall deliver the needy when he crieth;
the poor also, and him that hath no helper.
He shall spare the poor and needy,
and shall save the souls of the needy.
PSALM 72:12–13

23

The beloved of the LORD
shall dwell in safety by him;
and the LORD shall cover him all the day long,
and he shall dwell between his shoulders.

DEUTERONOMY 33:12

24

Then Jesus beholding him loved him,
and said unto him, One thing thou lackest:
go thy way, sell whatsoever thou hast,
and give to the poor,
and thou shalt have treasure in heaven:
and come, take up the cross, and follow me.

MARK 10:21

25

Though I walk in the midst of trouble,
thou wilt revive me: thou shalt stretch forth
thine hand against the wrath of mine enemies,
and thy right hand shall save me.

PSALM 138:7

26

And even to your old age I am he;
and even to hoar hairs will I carry you:
I have made, and I will bear;
even I will carry, and will deliver you.

ISAIAH 46:4

27

Peace I leave with you, my peace I give unto you:
not as the world giveth, give I unto you.
Let not your heart be troubled,
neither let it be afraid.
JOHN 14:27

28

Faith cometh by hearing,
and hearing by the word of God.
ROMANS 10:17

29

And he will love thee,
and bless thee, and multiply thee:
he will also bless the fruit of thy womb,
and the fruit of thy land, thy corn, and thy wine,
and thine oil, the increase of thy kine,
and the flocks of thy sheep,
in the land which he sware
unto thy fathers to give thee.

DEUTERONOMY 7:13

30

And, behold, I am with thee,
and will keep thee in all places whither thou
goest, and will bring thee again into this land;
for I will not leave thee, until I have done
that which I have spoken to thee of.

GENESIS 28:15

31

A false balance is abomination to the LORD:
but a just weight is his delight.

PROVERBS 11:1

32

The entrance of thy words giveth light;
it giveth understanding unto the simple.

PSALM 119:130

33

The father of the righteous shall greatly rejoice:
and he that begetteth a wise child
shall have joy of him.
Thy father and thy mother shall be glad,
and she that bare thee shall rejoice.
My son, give me thine heart,
and let thine eyes observe my ways.
PROVERBS 23:24–26

34

But God will redeem my soul from the power
of the grave: for he shall receive me.
PSALM 49:15

35

In my Father's house are many mansions:
if it were not so, I would have told you.
I go to prepare a place for you.
And if I go and prepare a place for you,
I will come again, and receive you unto myself;
that where I am, there ye may be also.

Joнn 14:2–3

36

For I the Lord thy God will hold thy right hand,
saying unto thee, Fear not; I will help thee.

Isaiah 41:13

37

For if ye forgive men their trespasses,
your heavenly Father will also forgive you.
MATTHEW 6:14

38

Herein is my Father glorified,
that ye bear much fruit;
so shall ye be my disciples.
JOHN 15:8

39

For the LORD your God is gracious and merciful,
and will not turn away his face from you,
if ye return unto him.
2 CHRONICLES 30:9

40

For ye have not received the spirit
of bondage again to fear;
but ye have received the Spirit of adoption,
whereby we cry, Abba, Father.
ROMANS 8:15

41

Whosoever therefore shall humble himself
as this little child, the same is greatest
in the kingdom of heaven.
MATTHEW 18:4

42

For this cause shall a man leave his father and
mother, and shall be joined unto his wife,
and they two shall be one flesh.

EPHESIANS 5:31

43

Blessed are the meek:
for they shall inherit the earth.

MATTHEW 5:5

44

And thou shalt do that which is right
and good in the sight of the LORD:
that it may be well with thee,
and that thou mayest go in and possess
the good land which the LORD
sware unto thy fathers.

DEUTERONOMY 6:18

45

And let us not be weary in well doing:
for in due season we shall reap, if we faint not.

GALATIANS 6:9

46

And he said unto them, Verily I say unto you,
There is no man that hath left house,
or parents, or brethren, or wife,
or children, for the kingdom of God's sake,
who shall not receive manifold more
in this present time, and in the world
to come life everlasting.

LUKE 18:29–30

47

He that is of a proud heart stirreth up strife:
but he that putteth his trust
in the LORD shall be made fat.
He that trusteth in his own heart is a fool:
but whoso walketh wisely, he shall be delivered.

PROVERBS 28:25–26

48

There hath no temptation taken you
but such as is common to man:
but God is faithful, who will not suffer you
to be tempted above that ye are able;
but will with the temptation also make a way
to escape, that ye may be able to bear it.

1 Corinthians 10:13

49

Heal me, O Lord, and I shall be healed;
save me, and I shall be saved:
for thou art my praise.

Jeremiah 17:14

50

And she shall bring forth a son,
and thou shalt call his name JESUS:
for he shall save his people from their sins.
MATTHEW 1:21

51

For thus saith the LORD unto the house of Israel,
Seek ye me, and ye shall live.
AMOS 5:4

52

For thou, LORD, wilt bless the righteous;
with favour wilt thou compass
him as with a shield.
PSALM 5:12

53

He healeth the broken in heart,
and bindeth up their wounds.
PSALM 147:3

54

When thou liest down, thou shalt not be afraid:
yea, thou shalt lie down,
and thy sleep shall be sweet.
PROVERBS 3:24

55

For the LORD heareth the poor,
and despiseth not his prisoners.
PSALM 69:33

56

Ask, and it shall be given you; seek,
and ye shall find; knock,
and it shall be opened unto you:
for every one that asketh receiveth;
and he that seeketh findeth; and to him
that knocketh it shall be opened.
MATTHEW 7:7–8

57

He that trusteth in his riches shall fall:
but the righteous shall flourish as a branch.
PROVERBS 11:28

58

And I will have mercy upon her
that had not obtained mercy;
and I will say to them which were not my people,
Thou art my people; and they shall say,
Thou art my God.

HOSEA 2:23

59

For the grace of God that bringeth
salvation hath appeared to all men,
teaching us that, denying ungodliness and
worldly lusts, we should live soberly, righteously,
and godly, in this present world.

TITUS 2:11–12

60

Beloved, if God so loved us,
we ought also to love one another.
1 JOHN 4:11

61

The glory of young men is their strength:
and the beauty of old men is the grey head.
PROVERBS 20:29

62

He giveth power to the faint; and to them
that have no might he increaseth strength.
ISAIAH 40:29

63

For God so loved the world,
that he gave his only begotten Son,
that whosoever believeth in him
should not perish, but have everlasting life.
JOHN 3:16

64

For I will pour water upon him that is thirsty,
and floods upon thy dry ground:
I will pour my spirit upon thy seed,
and my blessing upon thine offspring.
ISAIAH 44:3

65

I am the vine, ye are the branches:
He that abideth in me, and I in him,
the same bringeth forth much fruit:
for without me ye can do nothing.

JOHN 15:15

66

In all thy ways acknowledge him,
and he shall direct thy paths.

PROVERBS 3:6

67

For the needy shall not always be forgotten:
the expectation of the poor
shall not perish for ever.

PSALM 9:18

68

Sing unto the LORD, praise ye the LORD:
for he hath delivered the soul of the poor
from the hand of evildoers.

JEREMIAH 20:13

69

I will abundantly bless her provision:
I will satisfy her poor with bread.

PSALM 132:15

70

And Jesus answering saith unto them,
Have faith in God.
For verily I say unto you,
That whosoever shall say unto this mountain,
Be thou removed, and be thou cast into the sea;
and shall not doubt in his heart,
but shall believe that those things
which he saith shall come to pass;
he shall have whatsoever he saith.

MARK 11:22–23

71

He will swallow up death in victory:
and the Lord God will wipe away tears
from off all faces.

ISAIAH 25:8

72

Thy dead men shall live,
together with my dead body shall they arise.
Awake and sing, ye that dwell in dust:
for thy dew is as the dew of herbs,
and the earth shall cast out the dead.

Isaiah 26:19

73

But I say unto you, Love your enemies,
bless them that curse you,
do good to them that hate you,
and pray for them which despitefully
use you, and persecute you;
that ye may be the children
of your Father which is in heaven:
for he maketh his sun to rise on the evil
and on the good, and sendeth rain
on the just and on the unjust.

Matthew 5:44–45

74

And the work of righteousness shall be peace;
and the effect of righteousness quietness
and assurance for ever.

ISAIAH 32:17

75

As it is written, Behold, I lay in Sion
a stumblingstone and rock of offence: and
whosoever believeth on him shall not be ashamed.

ROMANS 9:33

76

The LORD will perfect that which concerneth me:
thy mercy, O LORD, endureth for ever:
forsake not the works of thine own hands.

PSALM 138:8

I love you so much,
Natasha!

77

For the LORD your God is he that goeth with you,
to fight for you against your enemies,
to save you.

DEUTERONOMY 20:4

78

Blessed is he that considereth the poor:
the LORD will deliver him in time of trouble.
The LORD will preserve him, and keep him alive;
and he shall be blessed upon the earth:
and thou wilt not deliver him
unto the will of his enemies.

PSALM 41:1–2

79

He that hath my commandments,
and keepeth them, he it is that loveth me:
and he that loveth me shall be loved of my Father,
and I will love him, and will
manifest myself to him.

JOHN 14:21

80

For he hath made him to be sin for us,
who knew no sin; that we might be made
the righteousness of God in him.

2 CORINTHIANS 5:21

81

For I will restore health unto thee,
and I will heal thee of thy wounds, saith the LORD.

JEREMIAH 30:17

82

In whom we have redemption through
his blood, the forgiveness of sins,
according to the riches of his grace.

EPHESIANS 1:7

83

For sin shall not have dominion over you:
for ye are not under the law,
but under grace.

ROMANS 6:14

84

By humility and the fear of the LORD are riches,
and honour, and life.

PROVERBS 22:4

85

Keep therefore the words of this covenant,
and do them, that ye may prosper in all that ye do.

DEUTERONOMY 29:9

86

Though he fall, he shall not be utterly cast down:
for the LORD upholdeth him with his hand.

PSALM 37:24

87

For the mountains shall depart,
and the hills be removed; but my kindness
shall not depart from thee, neither shall
the covenant of my peace be removed,
saith the LORD that hath mercy on thee.

ISAIAH 54:10

88

I am not ashamed of the gospel of Christ:
for it is the power of God unto salvation
to every one that believeth.

ROMANS 1:16

89

I have shewed you all things, how that so
labouring ye ought to support the weak,
and to remember the words of the Lord Jesus,
how he said, It is more blessed
to give than to receive.

Acts 20:35

90

And whosoever shall exalt himself
shall be abased; and he that shall humble
himself shall be exalted.

Matthew 23:12

91

The LORD openeth the eyes of the blind:
the LORD raiseth them that are bowed down:
the LORD loveth the righteous.

PSALM 146:8

92

But he that shall endure unto the end,
the same shall be saved.

MATTHEW 24:13

93

Blessed are ye, when men shall revile you,
and persecute you, and shall say all manner
of evil against you falsely, for my sake.
Rejoice, and be exceeding glad: for great is
your reward in heaven: for so persecuted
they the prophets which were before you.
MATTHEW 5:11–12

94

Every man also to whom God hath given riches
and wealth, and hath given him power to eat
thereof, and to take his portion, and to rejoice
in his labour; this is the gift of God.
ECCLESIASTES 5:19

95

And hope maketh not ashamed;
because the love of God is shed abroad in our
hearts by the Holy Ghost which is given unto us.
ROMANS 5:5

96

Blessed is the man that endureth temptation:
for when he is tried, he shall receive the crown
of life, which the Lord hath promised
to them that love him.
JAMES 1:12

97

The Lord is good unto them that wait for him,
to the soul that seeketh him.

LAMENTATIONS 3:25

98

Correct thy son, and he shall give thee rest;
yea, he shall give delight unto thy soul.

PROVERBS 29:17

99

Let no man say when he is tempted,
I am tempted of God: for God cannot be
tempted with evil, neither tempteth he any man.

JAMES 1:13

100

For whom the LORD loveth he correcteth;
even as a father the son in whom he delighteth.
PROVERBS 3:12

101

But now thus saith the LORD that created thee,
O Jacob, and he that formed thee, O Israel,
Fear not: for I have redeemed thee,
I have called thee by thy name;
thou art mine.
ISAIAH 43:1

102

Children's children are the crown of old men;
and the glory of children are their fathers.
PROVERBS 17:6

103

If any of you lacks wisdom, let him ask of God,
that giveth to all men liberally, and
upbraideth not; and it shall be given him.

JAMES 1:5

104

But whoso hearkeneth unto me shall dwell safely,
and shall be quiet from fear of evil.

PROVERBS 1:33

105

Let the wicked forsake his way,
and the unrighteous man his thoughts:
and let him return unto the LORD,
and he will have mercy upon him;
and to our God, for he will abundantly pardon.

ISAIAH 55:7

106

And I will put my spirit within you,
and cause you to walk in my statutes,
and ye shall keep my judgments, and do them.

Ezekiel 36:27

107

Beloved, let us love one another:
for love is of God; and every one that
loveth is born of God, and knoweth God.
He that loveth not knoweth not God;
for God is love.

1 John 4:7–8

108

Which executeth judgment for the oppressed:
which giveth food to the hungry.
The Lord looseth the prisoners.
PSALM 146:7

109

But seek ye first the kingdom of God,
and his righteousness;
and all these things shall be added unto you.
MATTHEW 6:33

110

And all things,
whatsoever ye shall ask in prayer,
believing, ye shall receive.
MATTHEW 21:22

111

For if these things be in you, and abound,
they make you that ye shall neither be barren
nor unfruitful in the knowledge
of our Lord Jesus Christ.
2 PETER 1:8

112

He that believeth on him is not condemned:
but he that believeth not is condemned already,
because he hath not believed in the name
of the only begotten Son of God.
JOHN 3:18

113

Now therefore hearken unto me, O ye children:
for blessed are they that keep my ways.
Hear instruction, and be wise,
and refuse it not.
PROVERBS 8:32–33

May you feel His nearness to
you xx

114

Yea, though I walk through the valley of the
shadow of death, I will fear no evil: for thou art
with me; thy rod and thy staff they comfort me.

PSALM 23:4

115

And they that know thy name will
put their trust in thee: for thou, LORD,
hast not forsaken them that seek thee.

PSALM 9:10

116

Lie not one to another, seeing that ye
have put off the old man with his deeds;
and have put on the new man,
which is renewed in knowledge after
the image of him that created him.

COLOSSIANS 3:9–10

117

For the LORD taketh pleasure in his people:
he will beautify the meek with salvation.

PSALM 149:4

118

That they do good, that they be rich
in good works, ready to distribute,
willing to communicate;
laying up in store for themselves
a good foundation against the time to come,
that they may lay hold on eternal life.

1 TIMOTHY 6:18–19

119

Therefore whosoever heareth these
sayings of mine, and doeth them,
I will liken him unto a wise man,
which built his house upon a rock:
and the rain descended, and the floods came,
and the winds blew, and beat upon that house;
and it fell not: for it was founded upon a rock.

MATTHEW 7:24–25

120

The name of the LORD is a strong tower:
the righteous runneth into it, and is safe.

PROVERBS 18:10

121

But if the wicked will turn from all his sins that
he hath committed, and keep all my statutes,
and do that which is lawful and right,
he shall surely live, he shall not die.
All his transgressions that he hath committed,
they shall not be mentioned unto him:
in his righteousness that he
hath done he shall live.

EZEKIEL 18:21–22

122

For this is good and acceptable
in the sight of God our Saviour;
who will have all men to be saved,
and to come unto the knowledge of the truth.

1 TIMOTHY 2:3–4

123

And I will send grass in thy fields for thy cattle,
that thou mayest eat and be full.

DEUTERONOMY 11:15

124

God is our refuge and strength,
a very present help in trouble.
Therefore will not we fear,
though the earth be removed,
and though the mountains
be carried into the midst of the sea.

PSALM 46:1–2

125

The holy scriptures, which are able
to make thee wise unto salvation
through faith which is in Christ Jesus.
All scripture is given by inspiration of God,
and is profitable for doctrine, for reproof,
for correction, for instruction in righteousness.
2 TIMOTHY 3:15–16

126

If they obey and serve him,
they shall spend their days in prosperity,
and their years in pleasures.
JOB 36:11

127

And we know that all things work together
for good to them that love God,
to them who are the called
according to his purpose.
ROMANS 8:28

128

And it shall come to pass,
that before they call,
I will answer;
and while they are yet speaking,
I will hear.
ISAIAH 65:24

129

This book of the law shall not depart
out of thy mouth; but thou shalt meditate
therein day and night, that thou mayest observe
to do according to all that is written therein:
for then thou shalt make thy way prosperous,
and then thou shalt have good success.

JOSHUA 1:8

130

Trust in the LORD, and do good;
so shalt thou dwell in the land,
and verily thou shalt be fed.
Delight thyself also in the LORD;
and he shall give thee the desires of thine heart.
Commit thy way unto the LORD;
trust also in him; and he shall bring it to pass.

PSALM 37:3–5

131

If ye be reproached for the name of Christ,
happy are ye; for the spirit of glory and
of God resteth upon you: on their part he is
evil spoken of, but on your part he is glorified.

1 PETER 4:14

132

And ye shall serve the LORD your God,
and he shall bless thy bread, and thy water;
and I will take sickness away
from the midst of thee.

EXODUS 23:25

133

For the LORD God is a sun and shield:
the LORD will give grace and glory:
no good thing will he withhold from
them that walk uprightly.

PSALM 84:11

134

And the peace of God,
which passeth all understanding,
shall keep your hearts and minds
through Christ Jesus.

PHILIPPIANS 4:7

135

But the mercy of the LORD is from everlasting
to everlasting upon them that fear him,
and his righteousness unto children's children.

PSALM 103:17

136

I love them that love me;
and those that seek me early shall find me.

PROVERBS 8:17

137

I will not leave you comfortless:
I will come to you.

JOHN 14:18

138

Love not sleep, lest thou come to poverty;
open thine eyes, and thou
shalt be satisfied with bread.

PROVERBS 20:13

139

Light is sown for the righteous,
and gladness for the upright in heart.
Rejoice in the LORD, ye righteous; and give
thanks at the remembrance of his holiness.

PSALM 97:11–12

140

Be of good courage, and he shall strengthen
your heart, all ye that hope in the LORD.

PSALM 31:24

141

No weapon that is formed against thee shall
prosper; and every tongue that shall rise
against thee in judgment thou shalt condemn.
This is the heritage of the servants of the LORD,
and their righteousness is of me, saith the LORD.
ISAIAH 54:17

142

Know therefore that the LORD thy God,
he is God, the faithful God,
which keepeth covenant and mercy
with them that love him and keep his
commandments to a thousand generations.
DEUTERONOMY 7:9

143

I will abundantly bless her provision:
I will satisfy her poor with bread.
PSALM 132:15

144

And he shall be like a tree planted
by the rivers of water,
that bringeth forth his fruit in his season;
his leaf also shall not wither;
and whatsoever he doeth shall prosper.
PSALM 1:3

145

Nevertheless I am continually with thee:
thou hast holden me by my right hand.
Thou shalt guide me with thy counsel,
and afterward receive me to glory.
PSALM 73:23–24

146

If we confess our sins,
he is faithful and just to forgive us our sins,
and to cleanse us from all unrighteousness.
1 JOHN 1:9

Thank you for loving Christ

147

My flesh and my heart faileth:
but God is the strength of my heart,
and my portion for ever.
PSALM 73:26

148

Surely he scorneth the scorners:
but he giveth grace unto the lowly.
PROVERBS 3:34

149

Ye shall walk in all the ways which the LORD
your God hath commanded you, that ye may live,
and that it may be well with you,
and that ye may prolong your days
in the land which ye shall possess.

DEUTERONOMY 5:33

150

Train up a child in the way he should go:
and when he old, he will not depart from it.

PROVERBS 22:6

151

But without faith it is impossible to please him:
for he that cometh to God must believe that he is,
and that he is a rewarder of them
that diligently seek him.

HEBREWS 11:6

152

Then will I sprinkle clean water upon you,
and ye shall be clean: from all your filthiness,
and from all your idols, will I cleanse you.
A new heart also will I give you, and
a new spirit will I put within you: and
I will take away the stony heart out of your flesh,
and I will give you an heart of flesh.

EZEKIEL 36:25–26

153

Fear not, little flock; for it is your
Father's good pleasure to give
you the kingdom.

LUKE 12:32

154

I will instruct thee and teach thee
in the way which thou shalt go:
I will guide thee with mine eye.

PSALM 32:8

155

Thou shalt be hid from
the scourge of the tongue:
neither shalt thou be afraid
of destruction when it cometh.
JOB 5:21

156

For the scripture saith,
Whosoever believeth on him
shall not be ashamed.
ROMANS 10:11

157

For we have not an high priest which cannot
be touched with the feeling of our infirmities;
but was in all points tempted like as we are,
yet without sin.
Let us therefore come boldly
unto the throne of grace,
that we may obtain mercy,
and find grace to help in time of need.
HEBREWS 4:15–16

158

The LORD shall preserve thee from all evil:
he shall preserve thy soul.
The LORD shall preserve thy going out
and thy coming in from this time forth,
and even for evermore.
PSALM 121:7–8

159

If ye then, being evil,
know how to give good gifts unto your children,
how much more shall your Father
which is in heaven give good things
to them that ask him?

MATTHEW 7:11

160

My brethren, count it all joy
when ye fall into divers temptations;
knowing this, that the trying
of your faith worketh patience.
But let patience have her perfect work,
that ye may be perfect and entire,
wanting nothing.

JAMES 1:2–4

161

The LORD thy God in the midst
of thee is mighty; he will save,
he will rejoice over thee with joy;
he will rest in his love,
he will joy over thee with singing.

ZEPHANIAH 3:17

162

He that loveth his brother abideth in the light,
and there is none occasion
of stumbling in him.

1 JOHN 2:10

163

Be not forgetful to entertain strangers:
for thereby some have
entertained angels unawares.
HEBREWS 13:2

164

He that walketh righteously,
and speaketh uprightly; he that despiseth
the gain of oppressions, that shaketh
his hands from holding of bribes,
that stoppeth his ears from hearing of blood,
and shutteth his eyes from seeing evil;
he shall dwell on high: his place of defence
shall be the munitions of rocks:
bread shall be given him;
his waters shall be sure.
ISAIAH 33:15–16

165

Behold, I will pour out my spirit unto you,
I will make known my words unto you.
PROVERBS 1:23

166

But the path of the just is as the shining light,
that shineth more and more
unto the perfect day.
PROVERBS 4:18

167

But love ye your enemies, and do good,
and lend, hoping for nothing again;
and your reward shall be great,
and ye shall be the children of the Highest:
for he is kind unto the unthankful and to the evil.
Be ye therefore merciful,
as your Father also is merciful.
Judge not, and ye shall not be judged:
condemn not, and ye shall not be condemned:
forgive, and ye shall be forgiven.

LUKE 6:35–37

168

Blessed be the LORD,
that hath given rest unto his people Israel,
according to all that he promised:
there hath not failed one word
of all his good promise.

1 KINGS 8:56

169

And God shall wipe away all tears from
their eyes; and there shall be no more death,
neither sorrow, nor crying,
neither shall there be any more pain:
for the former things are passed away.

REVELATION 21:4

170

Thy word is a lamp unto my feet,
and a light unto my path.

PSALM 119:105

171

He that hath pity upon the poor
lendeth unto the LORD;
and that which he hath given
will he pay him again.

PROVERBS 19:17

172

Children, obey your parents
in the Lord: for this is right.
Honour thy father and mother; which
is the first commandment with promise;
that it may be well with thee,
and thou mayest live long on the earth.

EPHESIANS 6:1–3

173

Cast thy burden upon the LORD,
and he shall sustain thee: he shall never
suffer the righteous to be moved.

PSALM 55:22

174

Let your conversation be without covetousness;
and be content with such things as ye have:
for he hath said, I will never leave thee,
nor forsake thee.

HEBREWS 13:5

175

For I am persuaded, that neither death, nor life,
nor angels, nor principalities, nor powers,
nor things present, nor things to come,
nor height, nor depth, nor any other creature,
shall be able to separate us from the love of God,
which is in Christ Jesus our Lord.
ROMANS 8:38–39

176

Be not afraid of sudden fear,
neither of the desolation of the wicked,
when it cometh.
For the LORD shall be thy confidence,
and shall keep thy foot from being taken.
PROVERBS 3:25–26

177

And ye shall eat in plenty, and be satisfied,
and praise the name of the LORD your God,
that hath dealt wondrously with you:
and my people shall never be ashamed.

JOEL 2:26

178

And every man that hath this hope
in him purifieth himself,
even as he is pure.

1 JOHN 3:3

179

And he said unto his disciples,
Therefore I say unto you,
Take no thought for your life, what ye shall eat;
neither for the body, what ye shall put on.
The life is more than meat,
and the body is more than raiment.

LUKE 12:22–23

180

The voice of rejoicing and salvation
is in the tabernacles of the righteous:
the right hand of the LORD doeth valiantly.

PSALM 118:15

181

Then he said unto them,
Go your way, eat the fat, and drink the sweet,
and send portions unto them
for whom nothing is prepared:
for this day is holy unto our Lord:
neither be ye sorry;
for the joy of the Lord is your strength.

NEHEMIAH 8:10

182

He becometh poor that dealeth with a slack hand:
but the hand of the diligent maketh rich.

PROVERBS 10:4

183

The meek will he guide in judgment:
and the meek will he teach his way.

PSALM 25:9

184

For the oppression of the poor,
for the sighing of the needy,
now will I arise, saith the LORD;
I will set him in safety from him
that puffeth at him.

PSALM 12:5

185

Peace, peace to him that is far off,
and to him that is near, saith the LORD;
and I will heal him.

ISAIAH 57:19

186

And this is the confidence that
we have in him, that, if we ask any thing
according to his will, he heareth us:
and if we know that he hear us,
whatsoever we ask, we know that we have
the petitions that we desired of him.

1 JOHN 5:14–15

187

But he was wounded for our transgressions,
he was bruised for our iniquities:
the chastisement of our peace was upon him;
and with his stripes we are healed.

ISAIAH 53:5

188

For God, who commanded the light to shine
out of darkness, hath shined in our hearts,
to give the light of the knowledge of the
glory of God in the face of Jesus Christ.

2 CORINTHIANS 4:6

189

If ye keep my commandments,
ye shall abide in my love;
even as I have kept my Father's
commandments, and abide in his love.

JOHN 15:10

190

Then shall ye call upon me,
and ye shall go and pray unto me,
and I will hearken unto you.

JEREMIAH 29:12

191

Verily, verily, I say unto you,
If a man keep my saying,
he shall never see death.

JOHN 8:51

192

Verily, verily, I say unto you,
He that heareth my word,
and believeth on him that sent me,
hath everlasting life,
and shall not come into condemnation;
but is passed from death unto life.

JOHN 5:24

193

For the word of God is quick, and powerful,
and sharper than any twoedged sword,
piercing even to the dividing asunder of soul
and spirit, and of the joints and marrow,
and is a discerner of the thoughts
and intents of the heart.

HEBREWS 4:12

194

And therefore will the LORD wait,
that he may be gracious unto you, and therefore
will he be exalted, that he may have mercy
upon you: for the LORD is a God of judgment:
blessed are all they that wait for him.
ISAIAH 30:18

195

A soft answer turneth away wrath:
but grievous words stir up anger.
PROVERBS 15:1

196

Then shalt thou call, and the LORD shall answer;
thou shalt cry, and he shall say, Here I am.
ISAIAH 58:9

197

For whosoever shall give you a cup
of water to drink in my name,
because ye belong to Christ,
verily I say unto you,
he shall not lose his reward.

MARK 9:41

198

Be of good courage,
and he shall strengthen your heart,
all ye that hope in the LORD.

PSALM 31:24

199

For thou art my hope, O Lord GOD:
thou art my trust from my youth.

PSALM 71:5